暴风雨要来了

Sharing the Planet | Non-Fiction Series

Copyright © 2022 by Level Learning, INC. and Washington Yu Ying PCS™
Original and Edited Text Copyright © 2022 by Washington Yu Ying PCS™

All rights reserved. No part of this book in whole or part may be reproduced without written permission from the publisher.

Published by Level Learning, INC.

Content Contributors:
Washington Yu Ying PCS™ - Qianyi (Shirley) Zhang, Pearl Zao He You
Level Learning - Jingyao Qi

Illustrations by: Josh Taira

Leveling classification based on Level Learning standard.
For full description, visit www.levellearning.com

ISBN 978-1-64040-050-4
Simplified Chinese Edition

About Level Learning:

Level Learning provides a literacy focused curriculum specifically designed for K-12 Chinese as a Second Language classrooms. Our program offers 20 levels of specific and detailed objectives, leveled texts and passages, mastery-based online assessment, and analytics to enable data-driven instruction. Level Learning reading curriculum for both literature and informational text emphasize grammar and comprehension skills to help teachers develop confident and independent Chinese language readers. The non-fiction series of books are specifically designed to support our informational text course based on multiple national standards. To learn more about our entire offering, visit www.levellearning.com.

About Washington Yu Ying PCS™:

Washington Yu Ying PCS is a Mandarin English dual language immersion International Baccalaureate (IB) World school. Yu Ying's mission is to inspire and prepare young people to create a better world by challenging them to reach their full potential in a nurturing Chinese/English educational environment. Yu Ying's comprehensive IB, dual immersion curriculum equips students with global competencies for success in the real world. As a leader in immersion education, Yu Ying is determined to advance Chinese language programs and global citizenry education by helping other schools create and strengthen their Chinese programs. For more information, email: products@washingtonyuying.org

暴风雨要来了,我们要做好准备。

快来看看我们准备了什么。

我们准备了食物。我们会有食物吃。

我们准备了水。我们会有水喝。

我们准备了蜡烛。天黑了，我们也能看得见。

我们修剪了树枝。风再大,我们的房子也是安全的。

我们还准备了书和玩具。

暴风雨要来了,我们都准备好了。

Glossary

	Pinyin	English Definition
暴风雨	bào fēng yǔ	storm
做	zuò	to do
好	hǎo	well, good
准备	zhǔn bèi	to prepare
食物	shí wù	food
喝	hē	to drink
蜡烛	là zhú	candle
修剪	xiū jiǎn	to trim
树枝	shù zhī	tree branch
房子	fáng zi	house
安全	ān quán	safe
玩具	wán jù	toy, game

www.ingramcontent.com/pod-product-compliance
Lightning Source LLC
Chambersburg PA
CBHW041224070526
44584CB00001B/91